THIS BOOK

BELONG TO

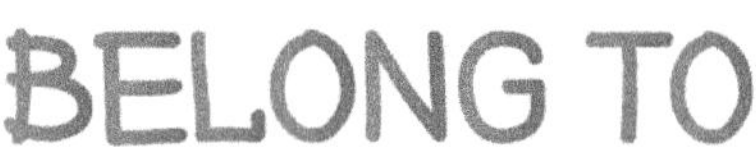

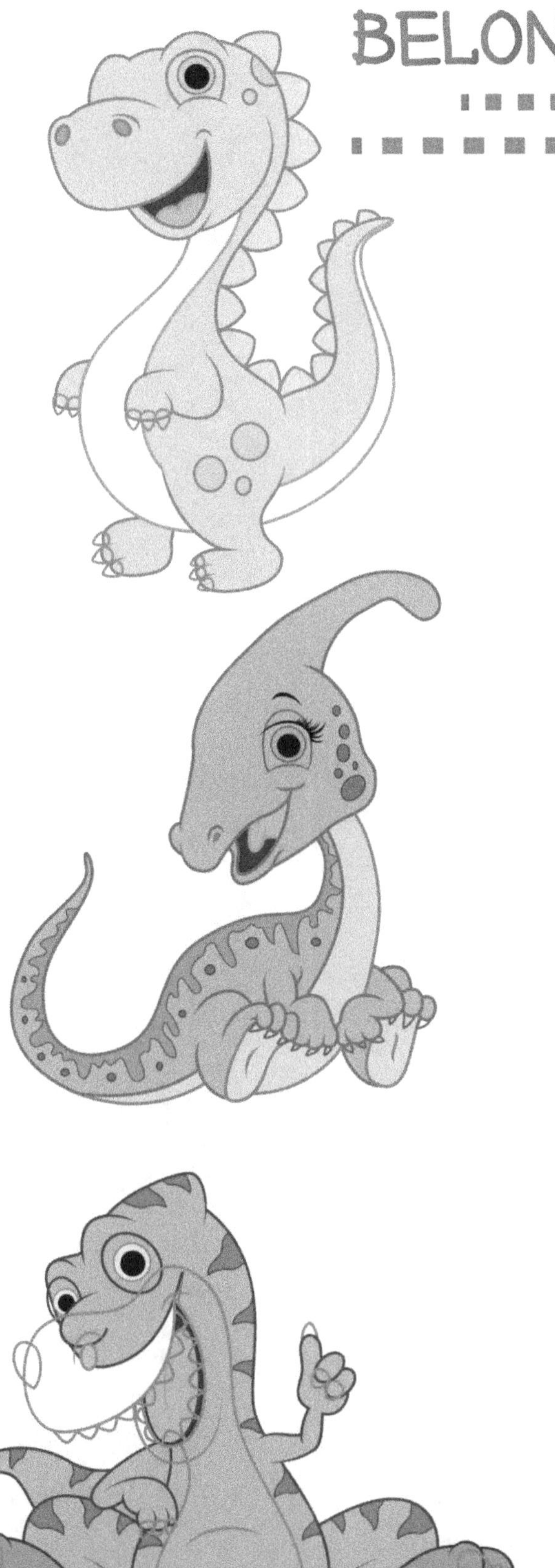

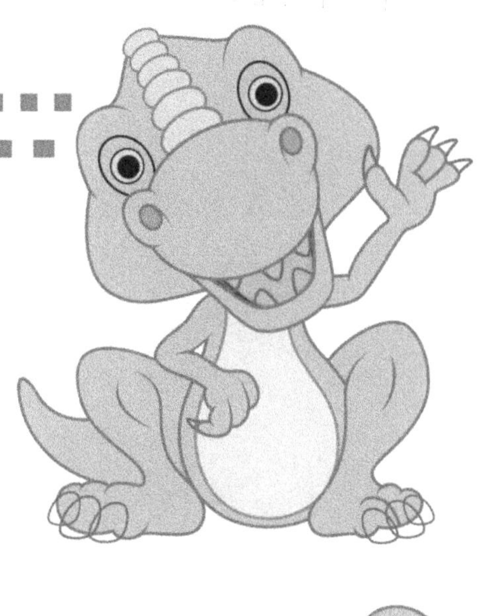

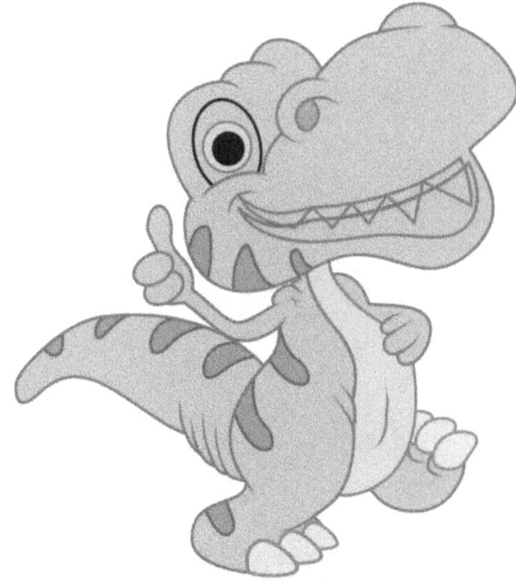

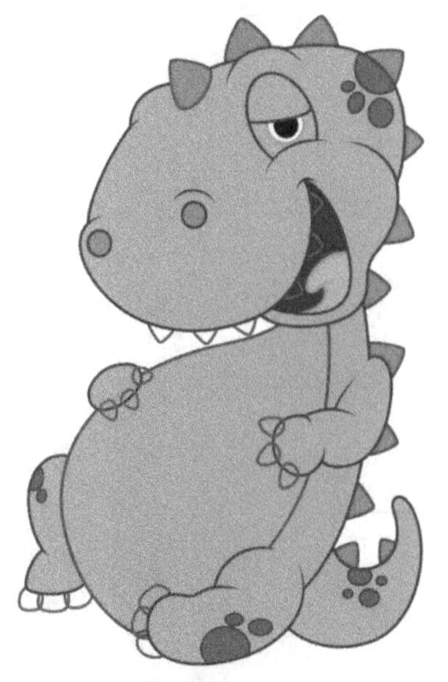

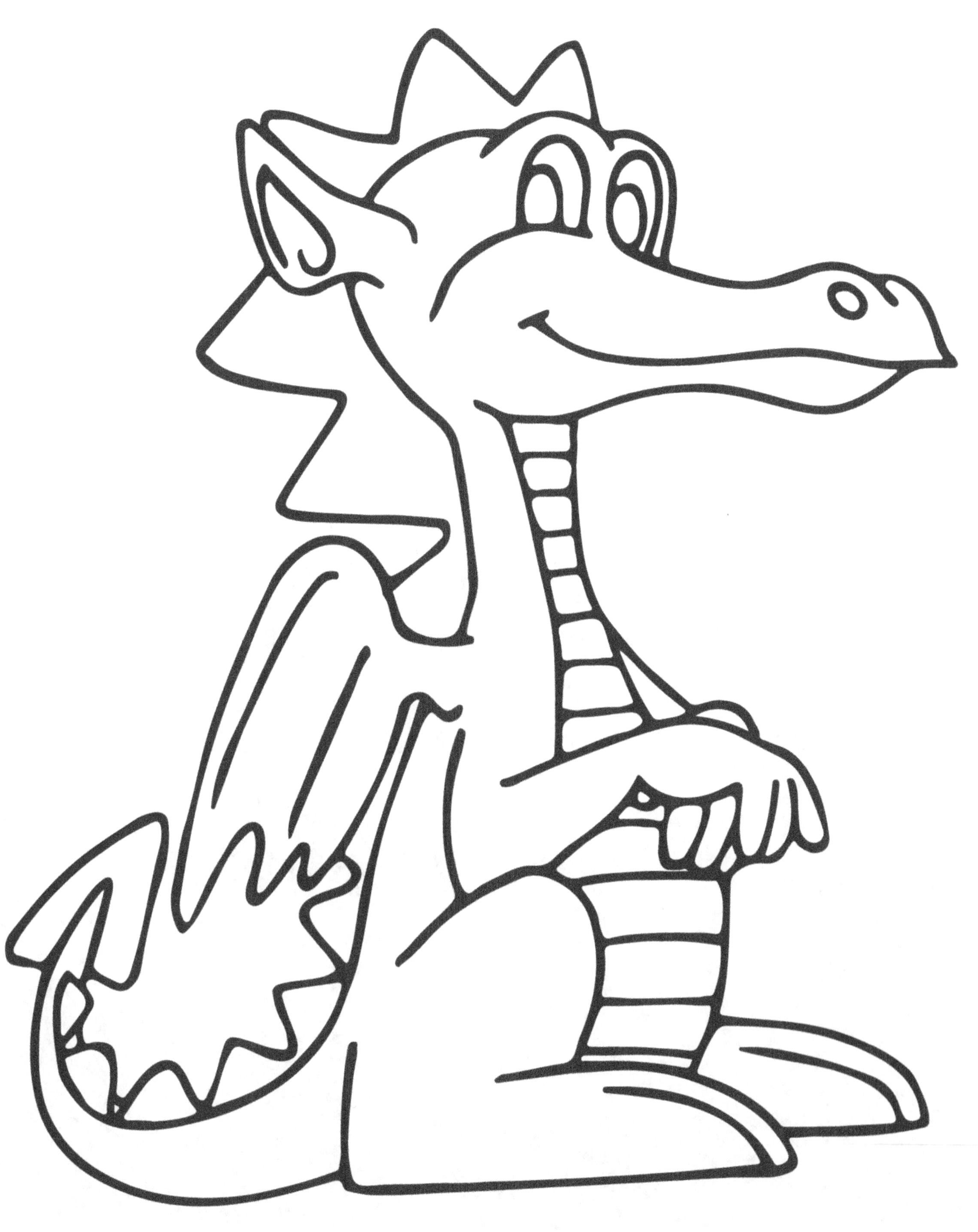

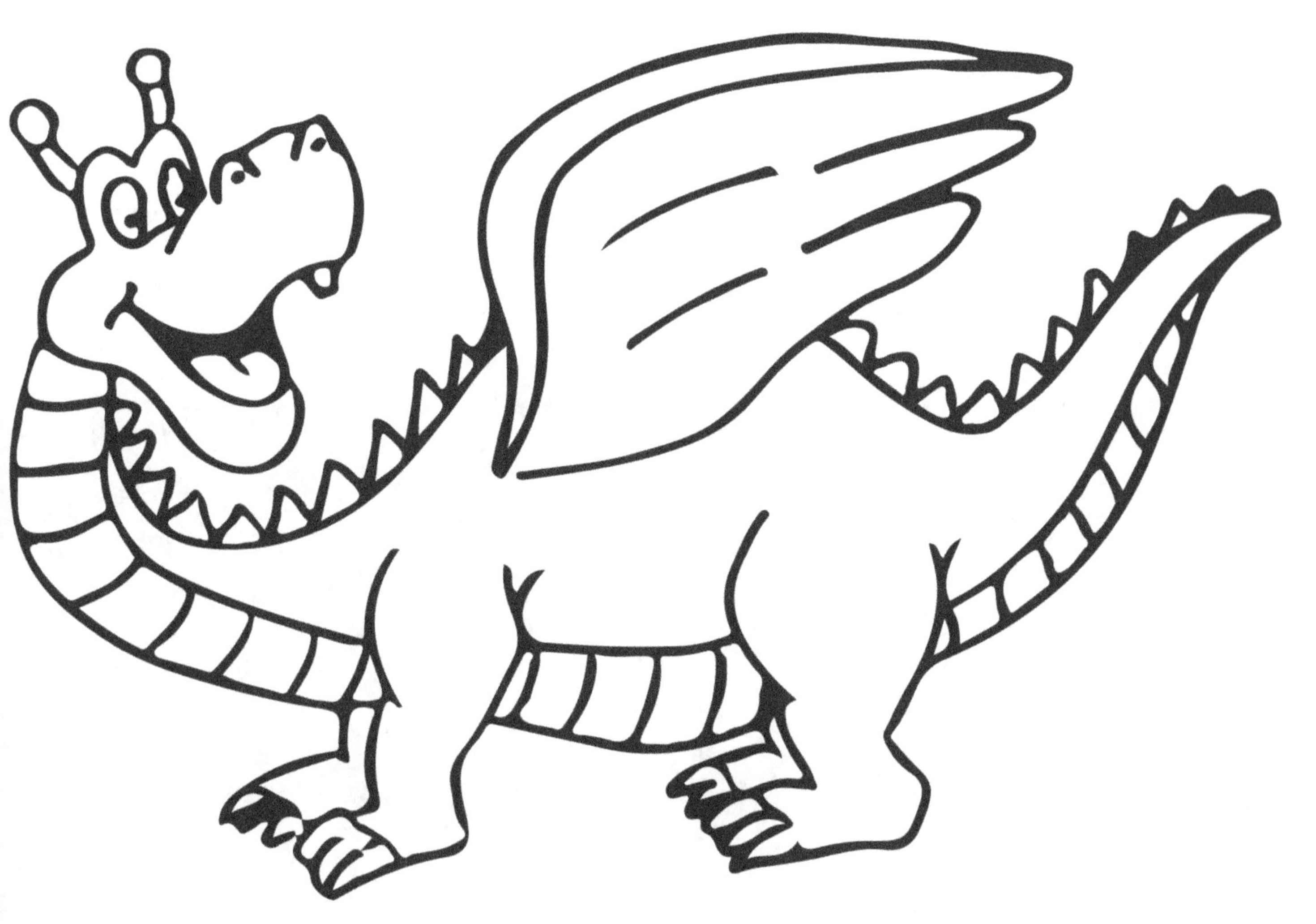

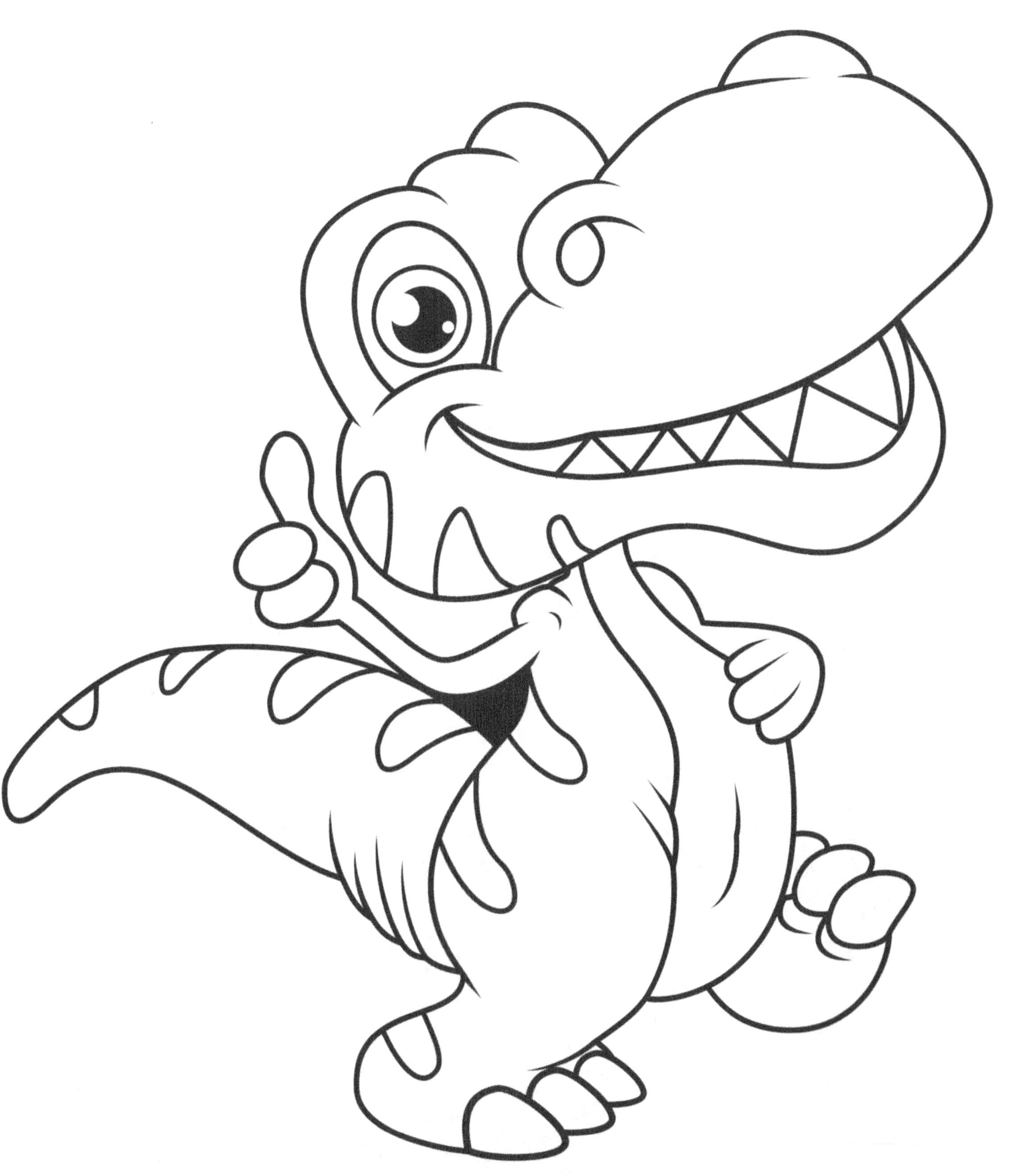

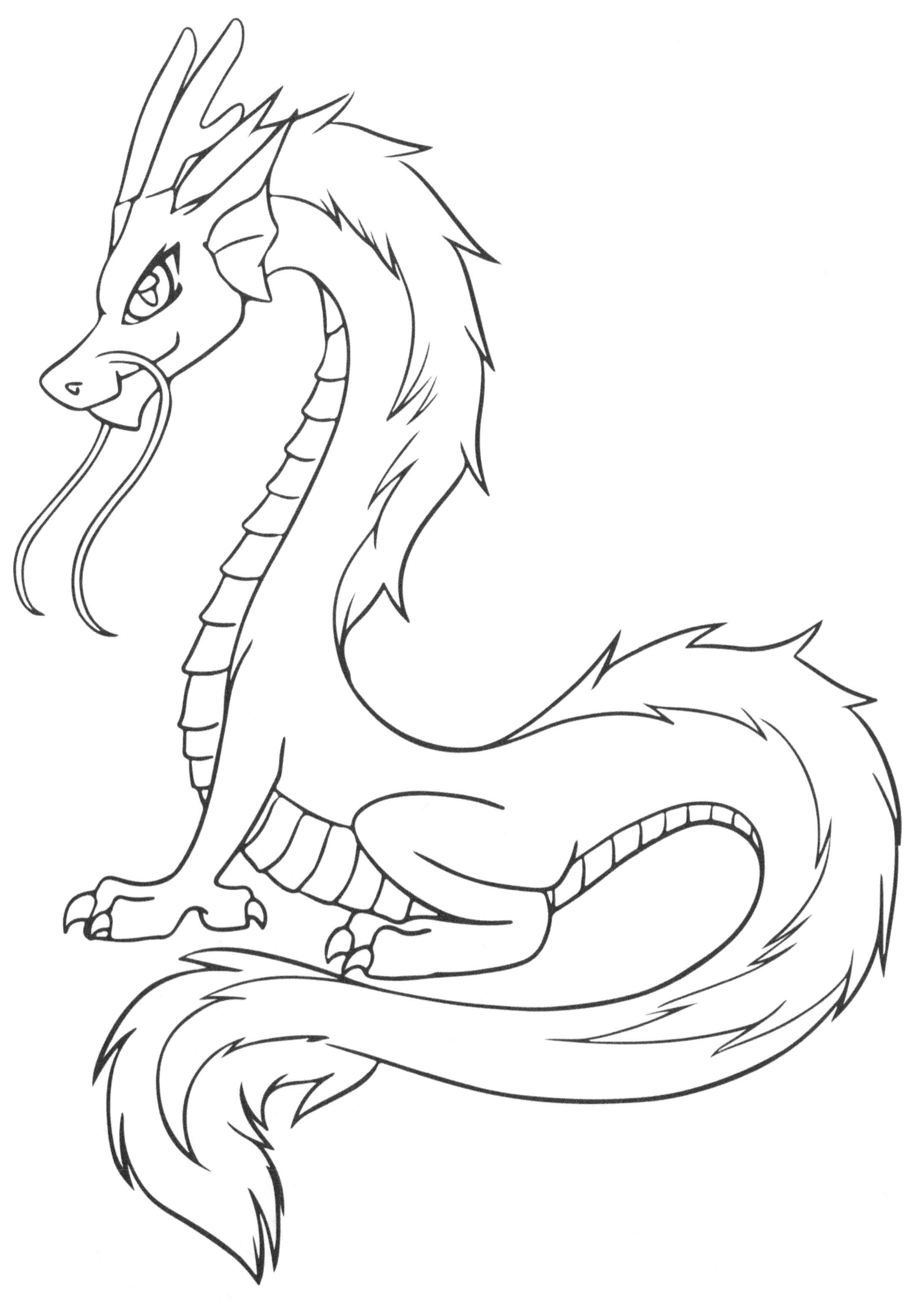

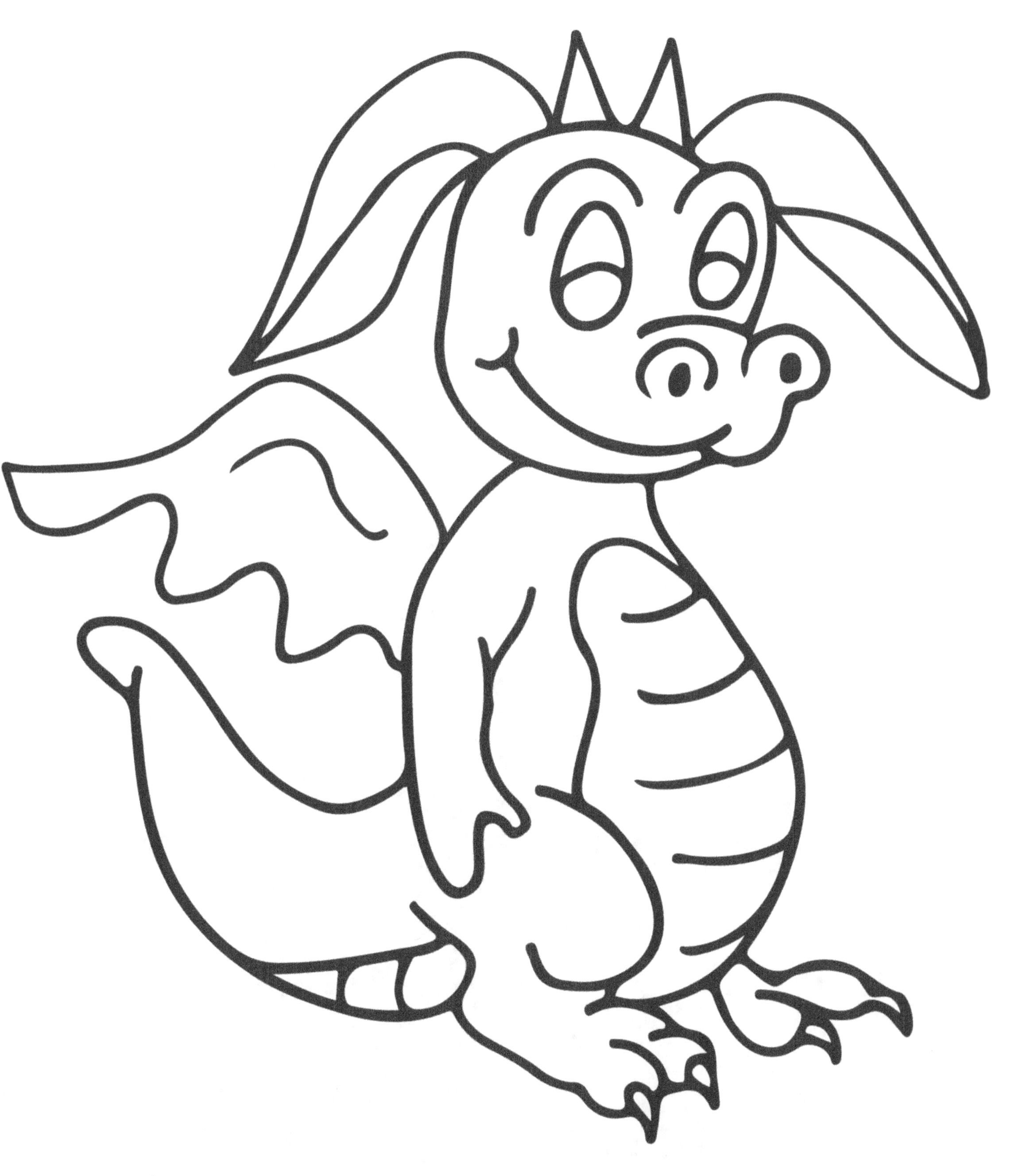

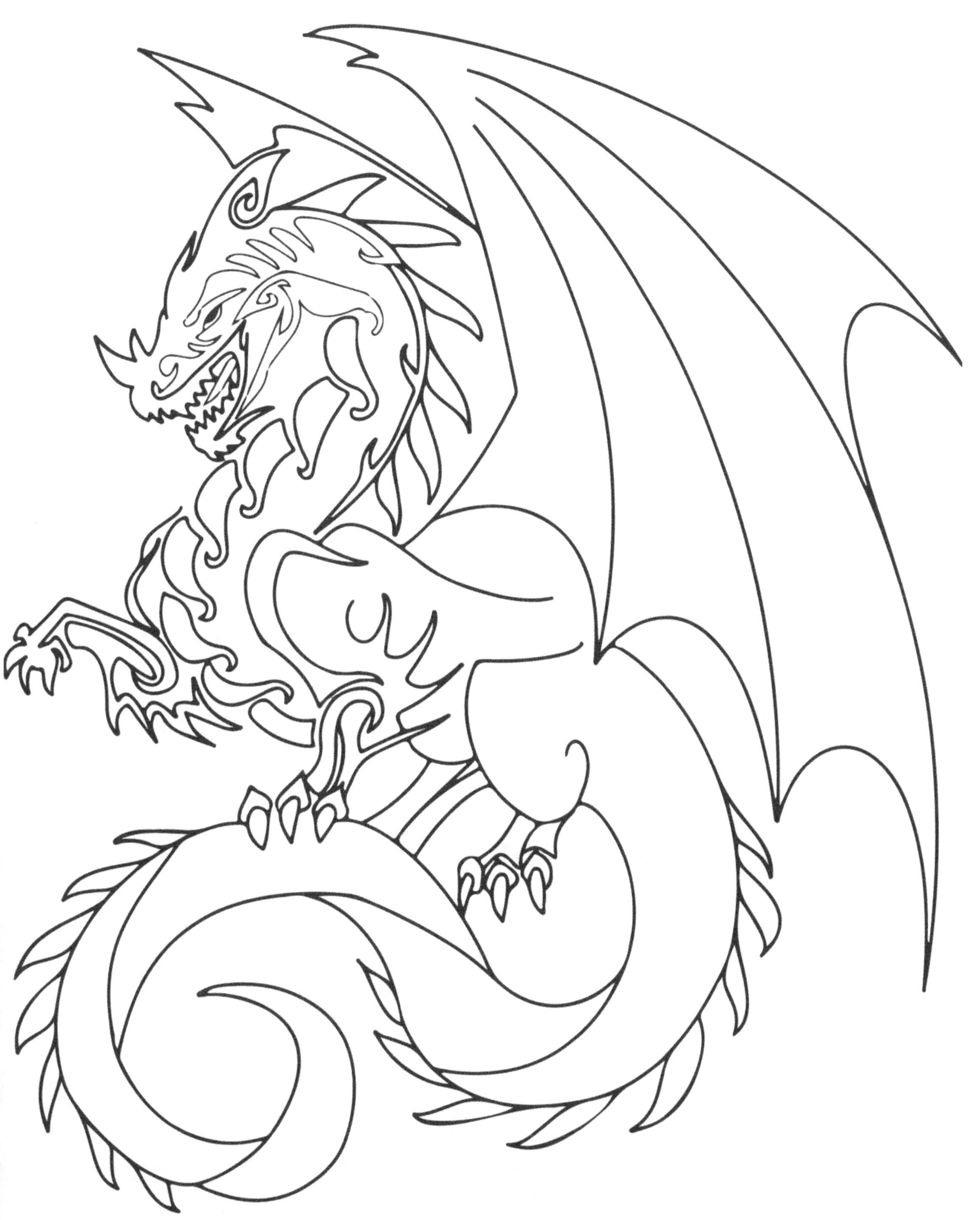

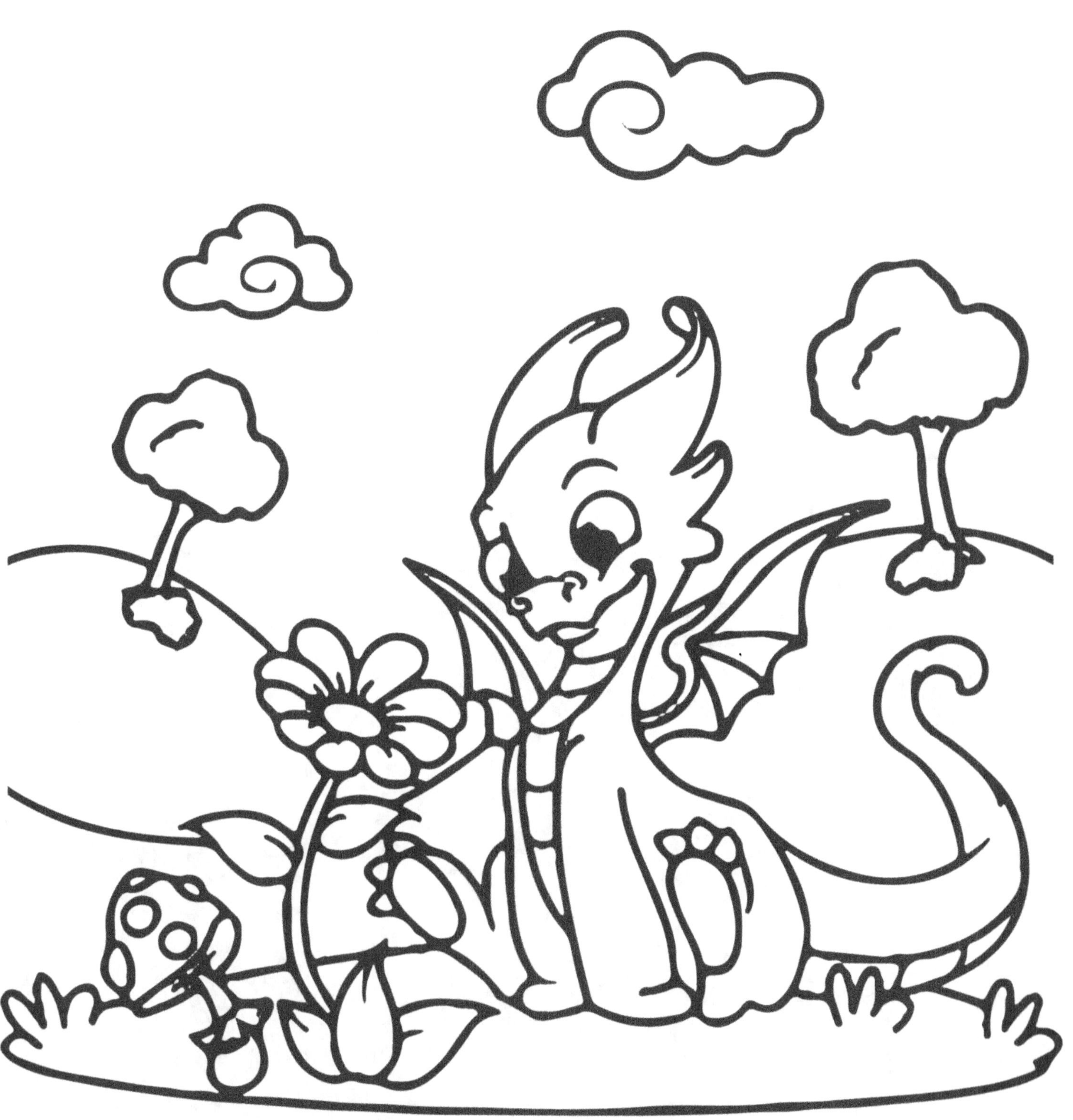

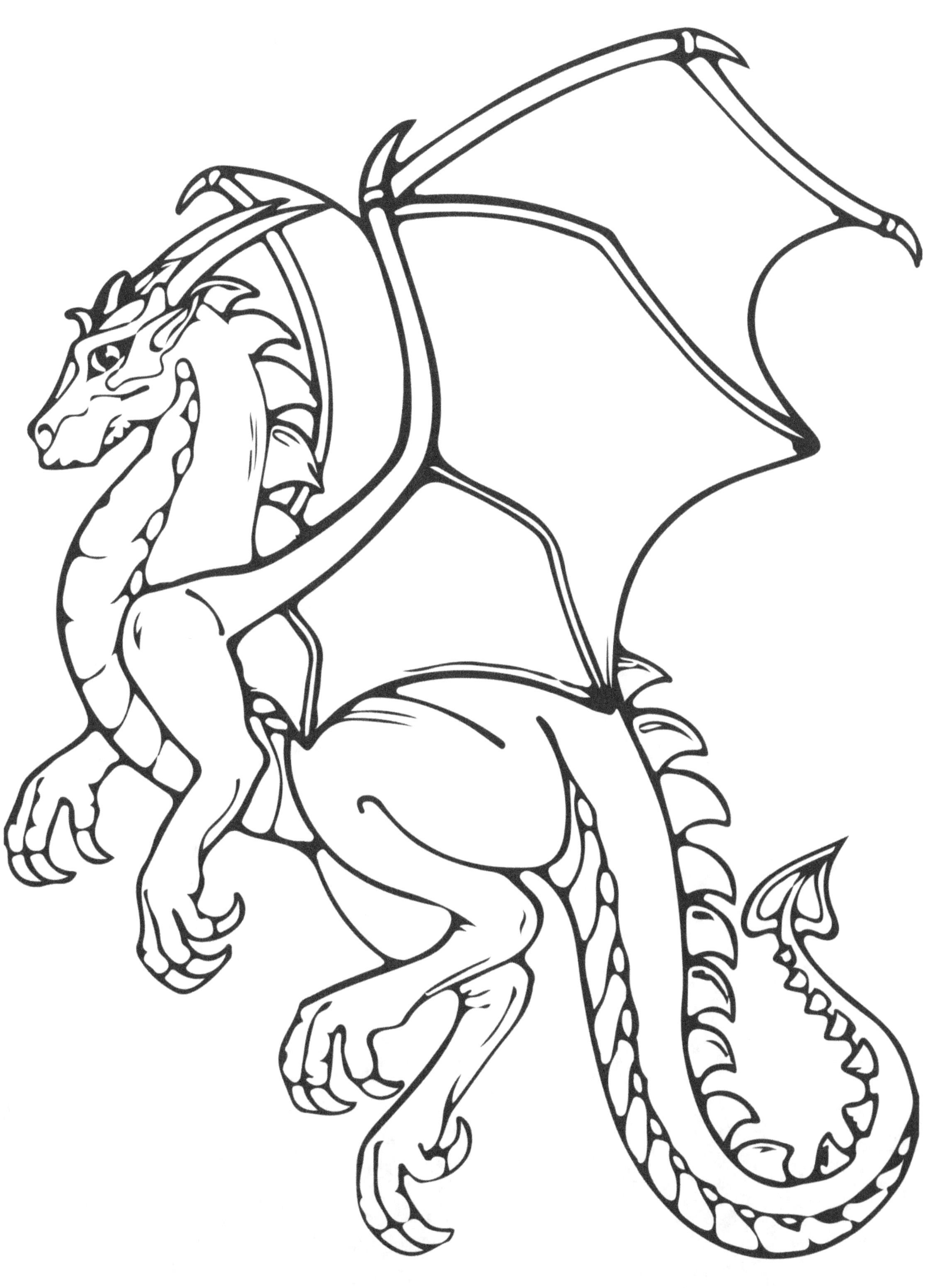

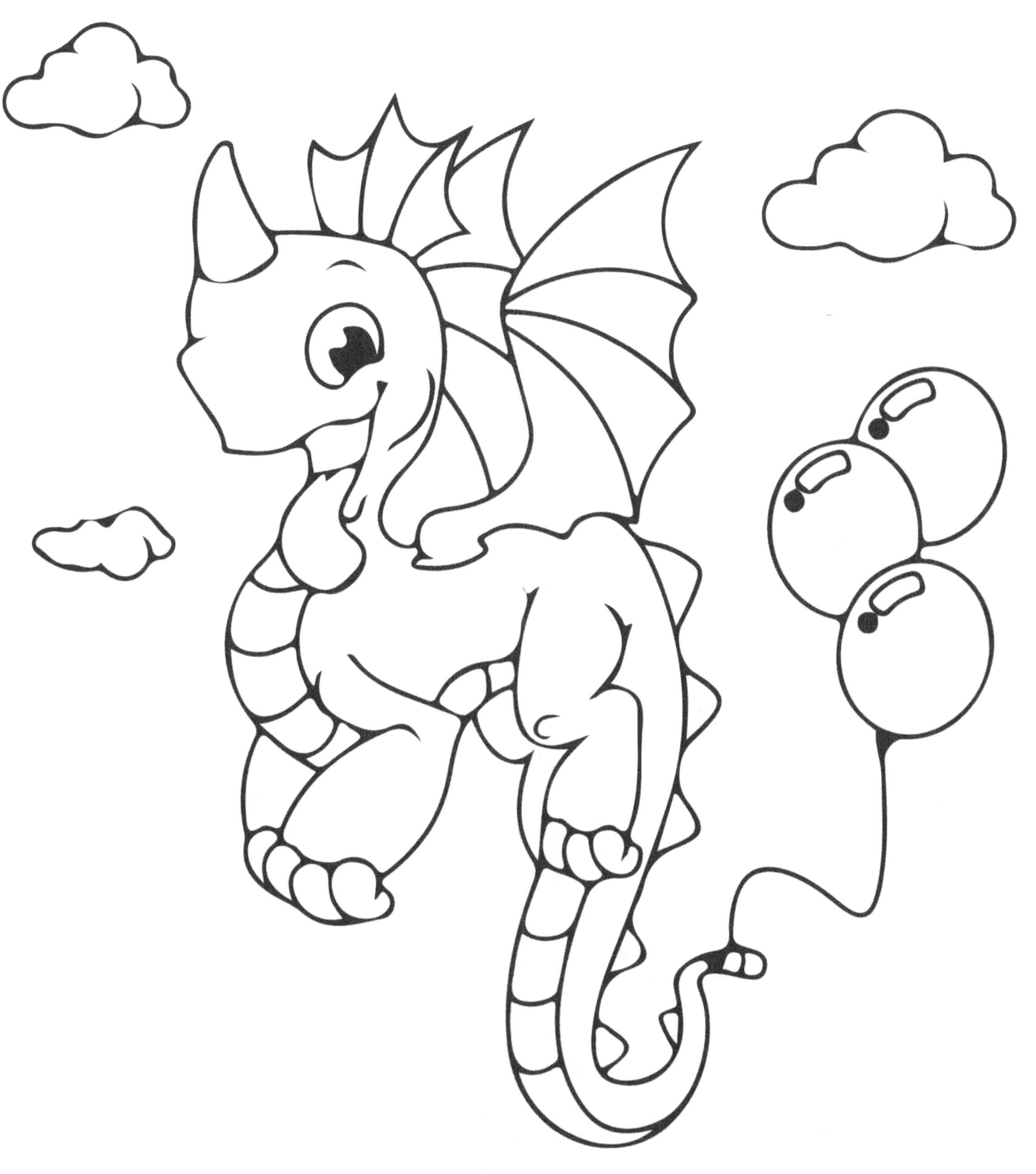

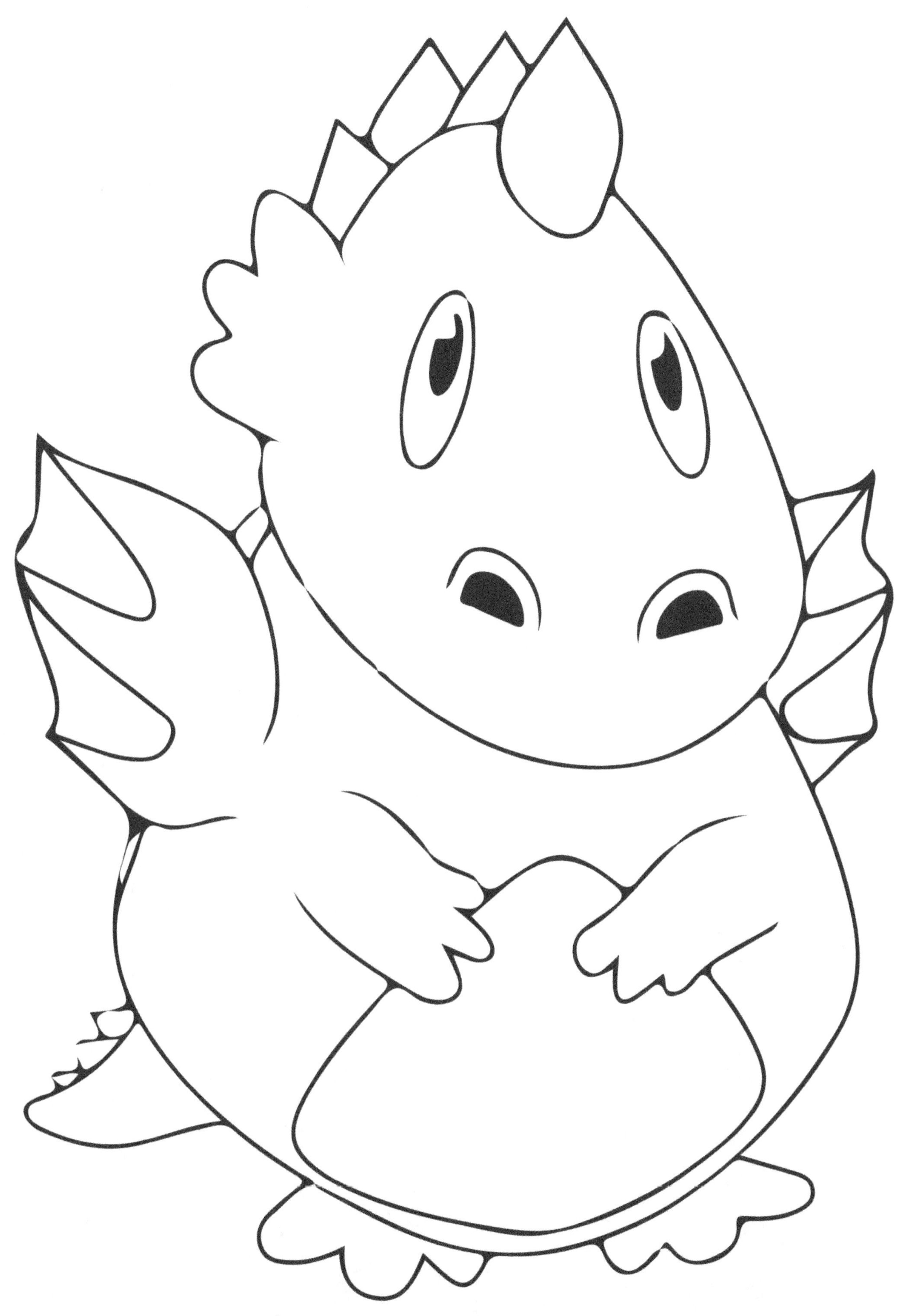

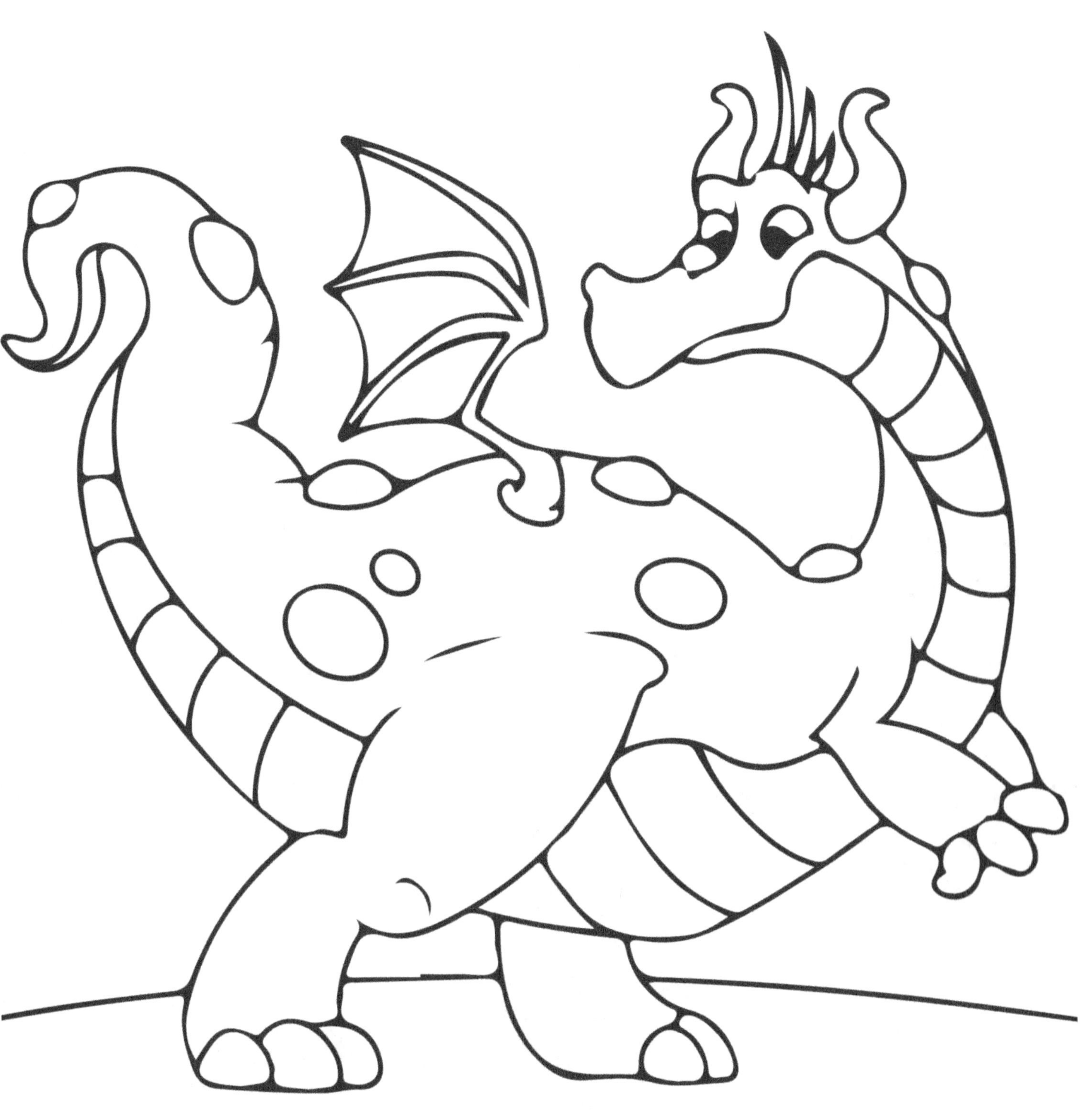

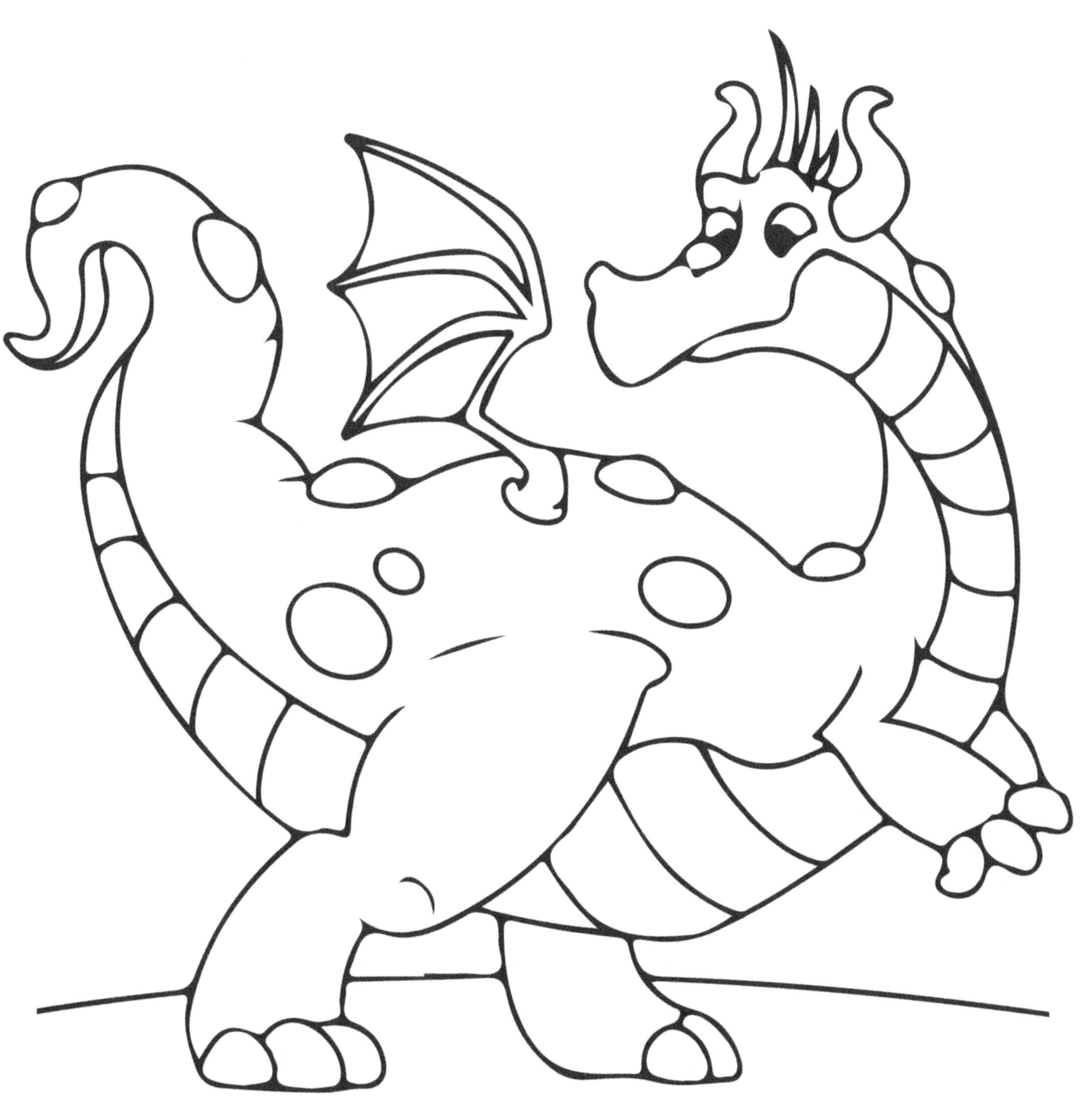

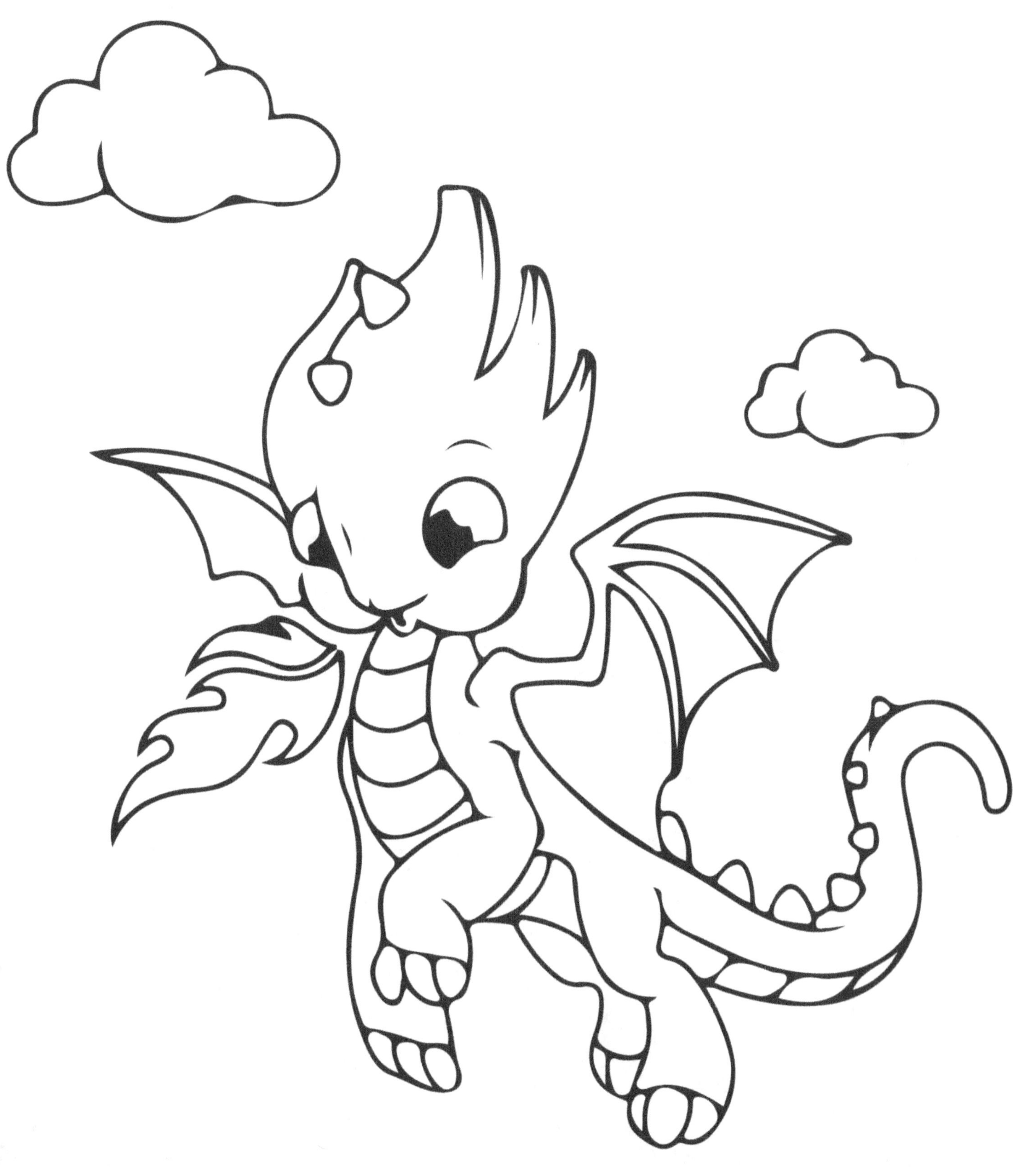

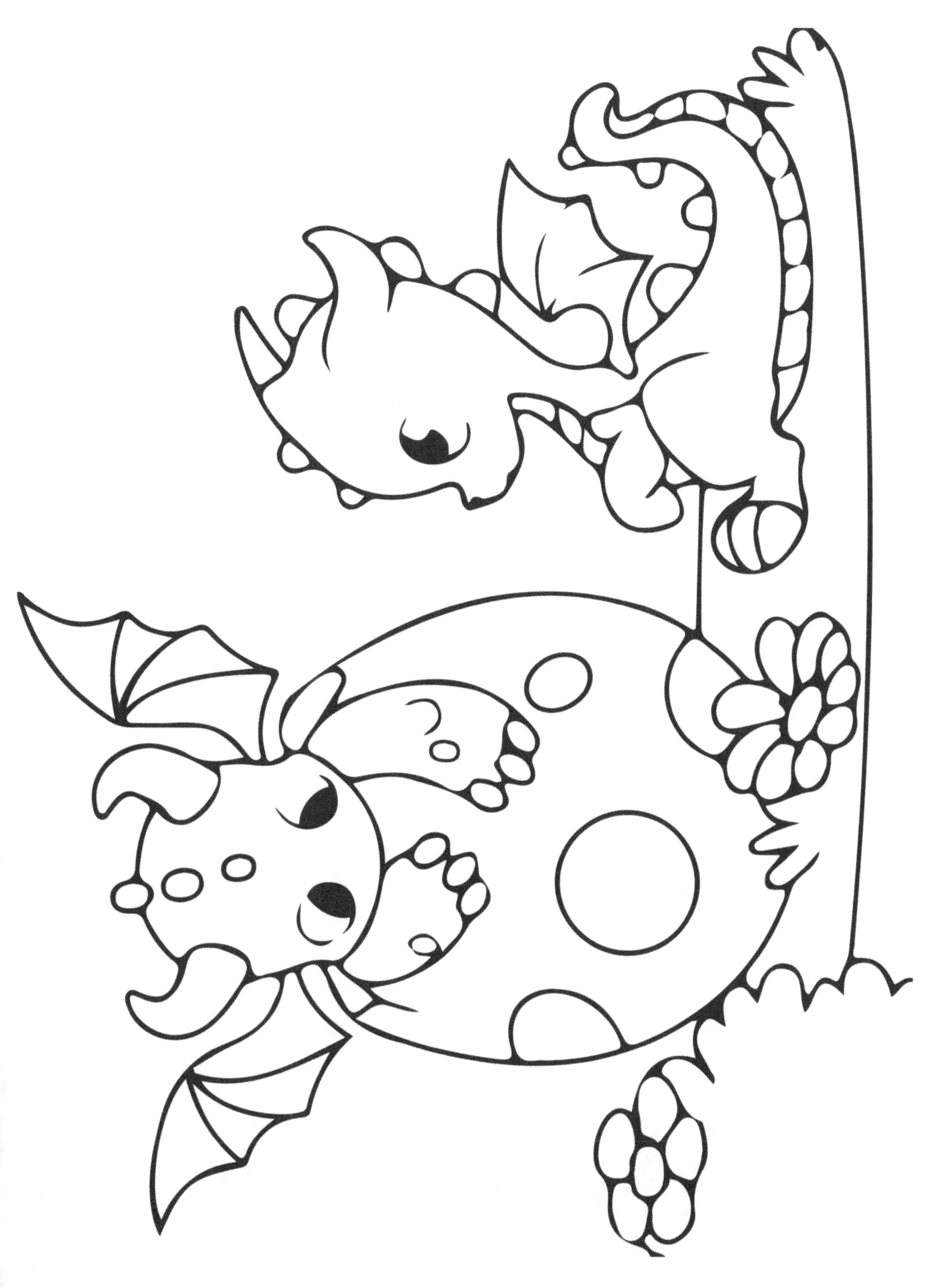

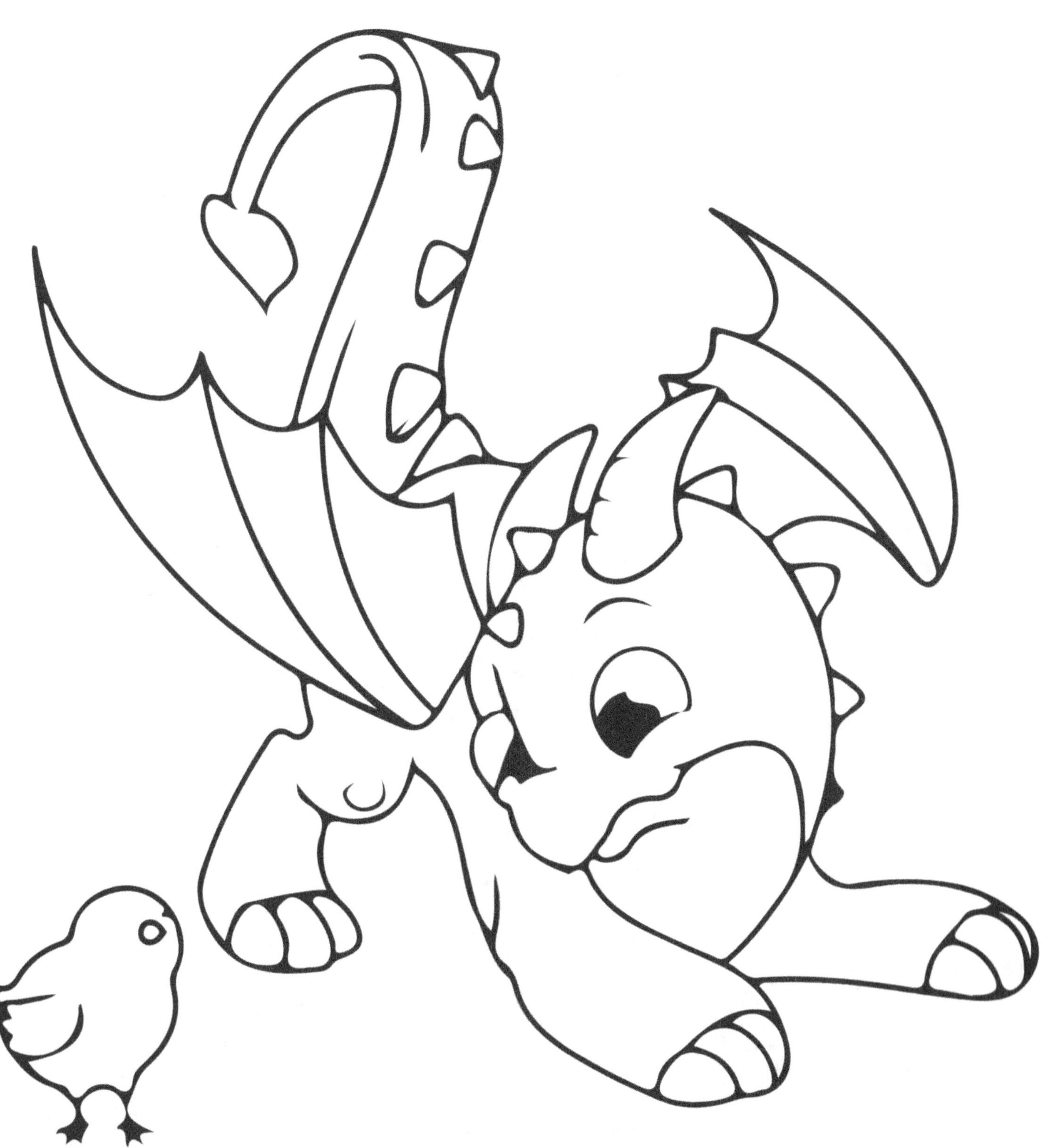

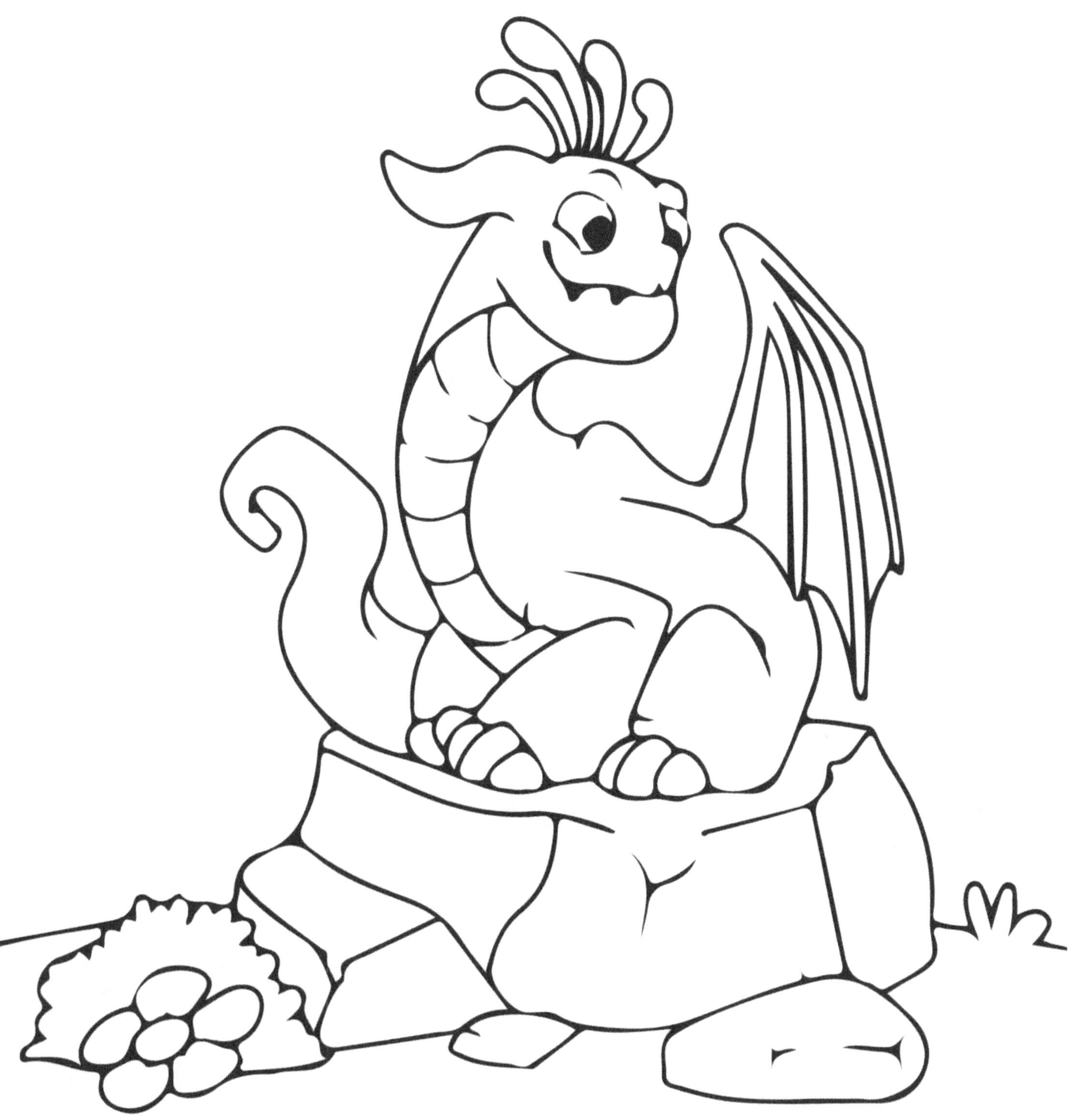

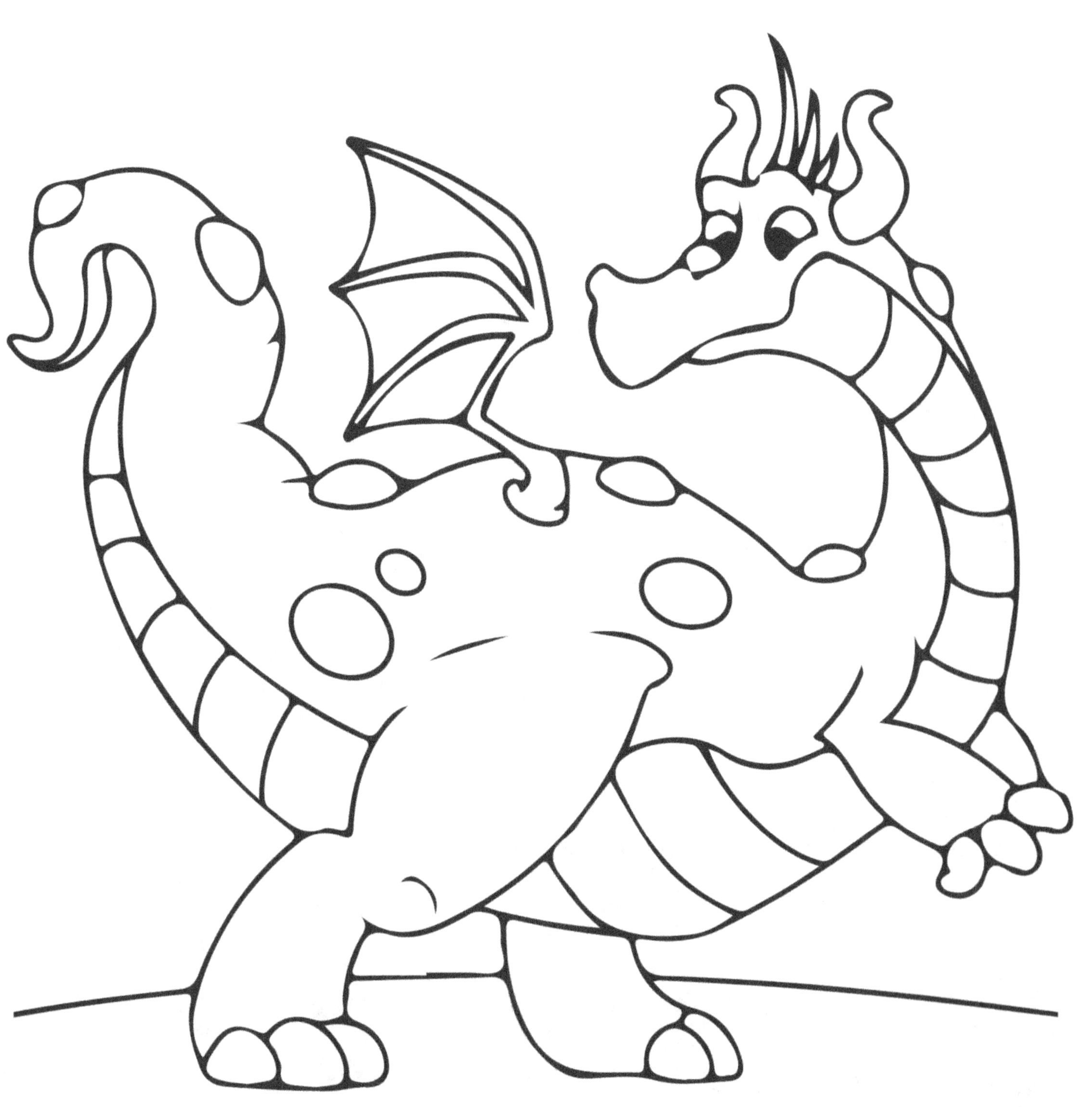

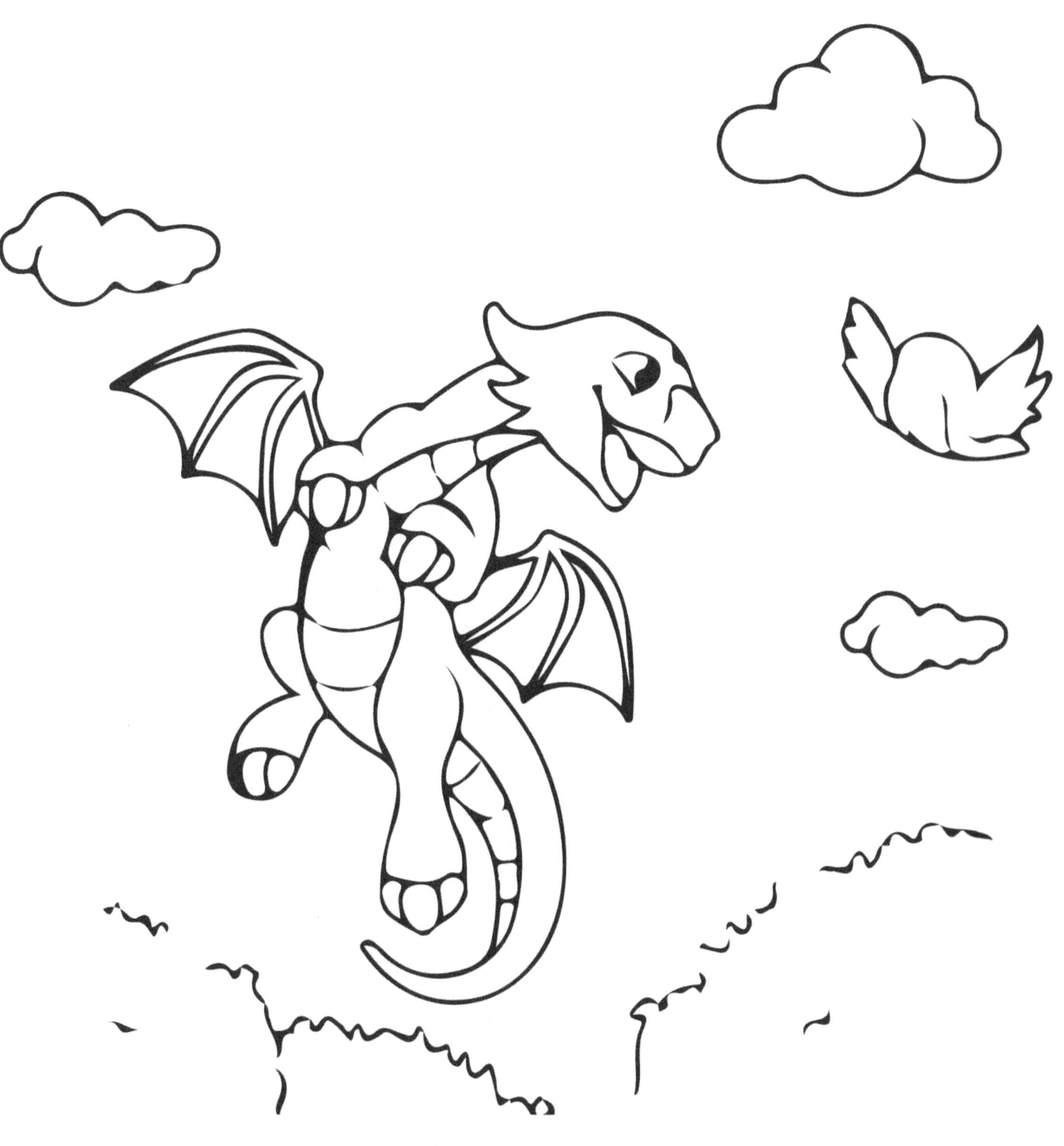

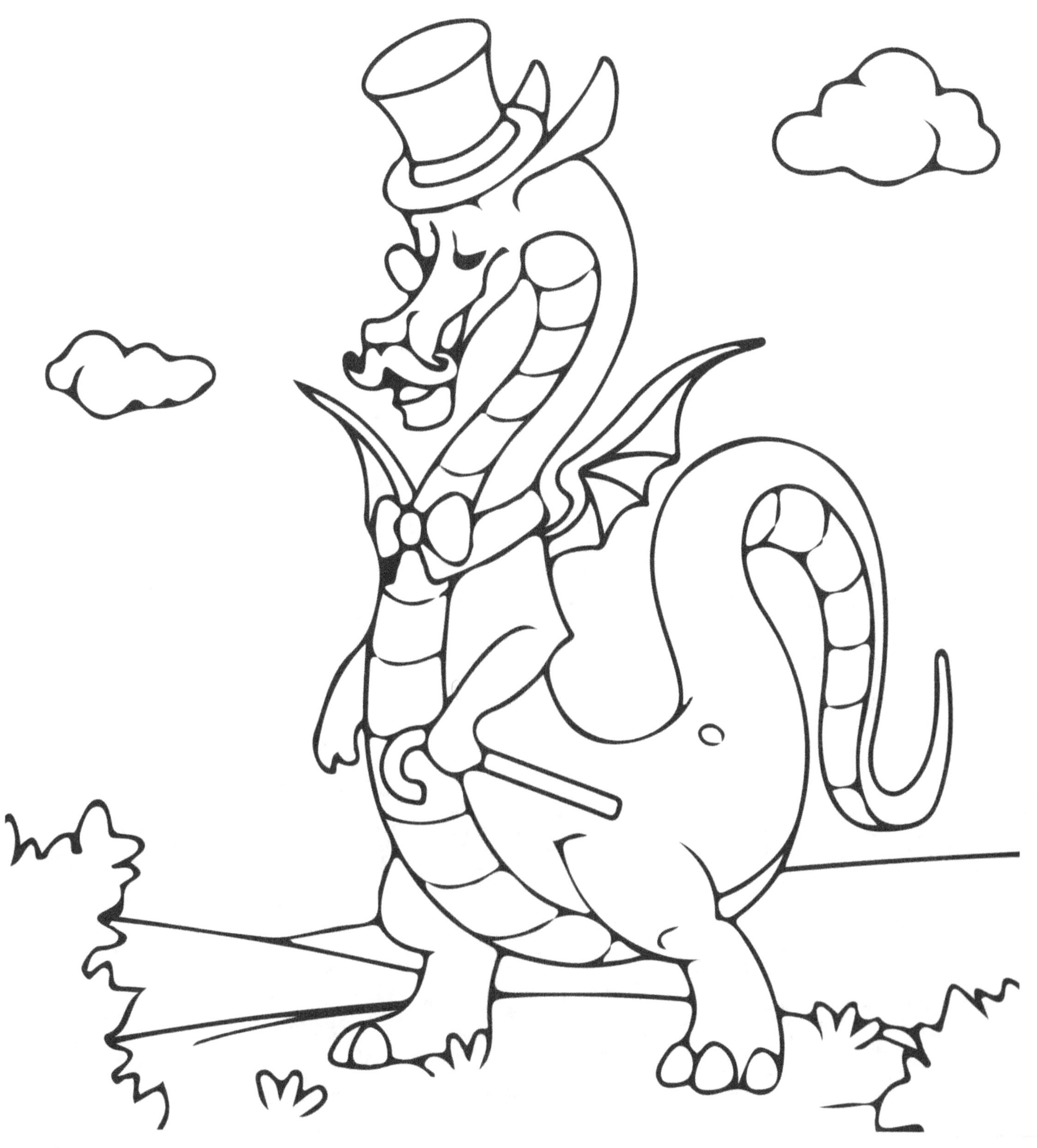

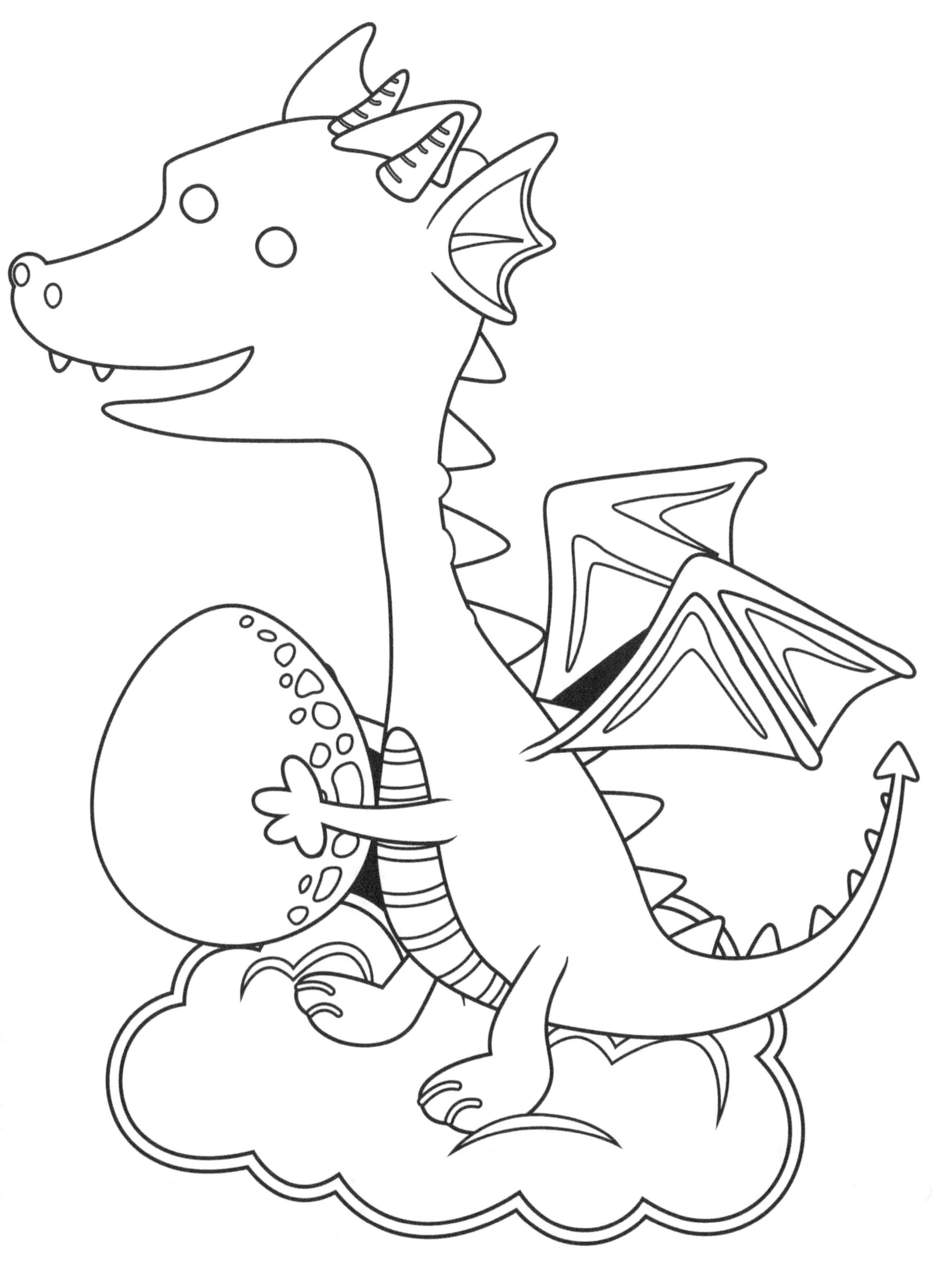

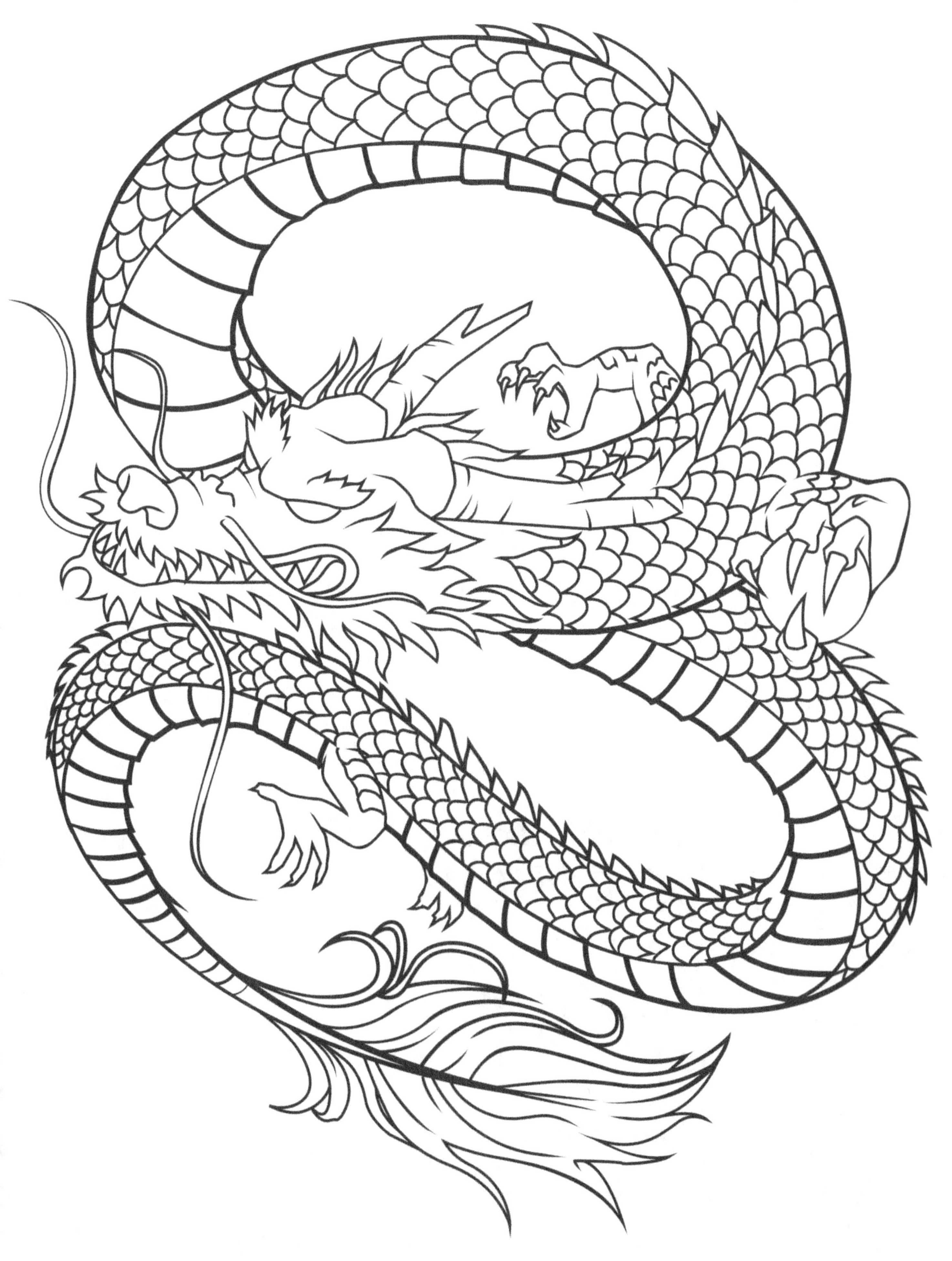

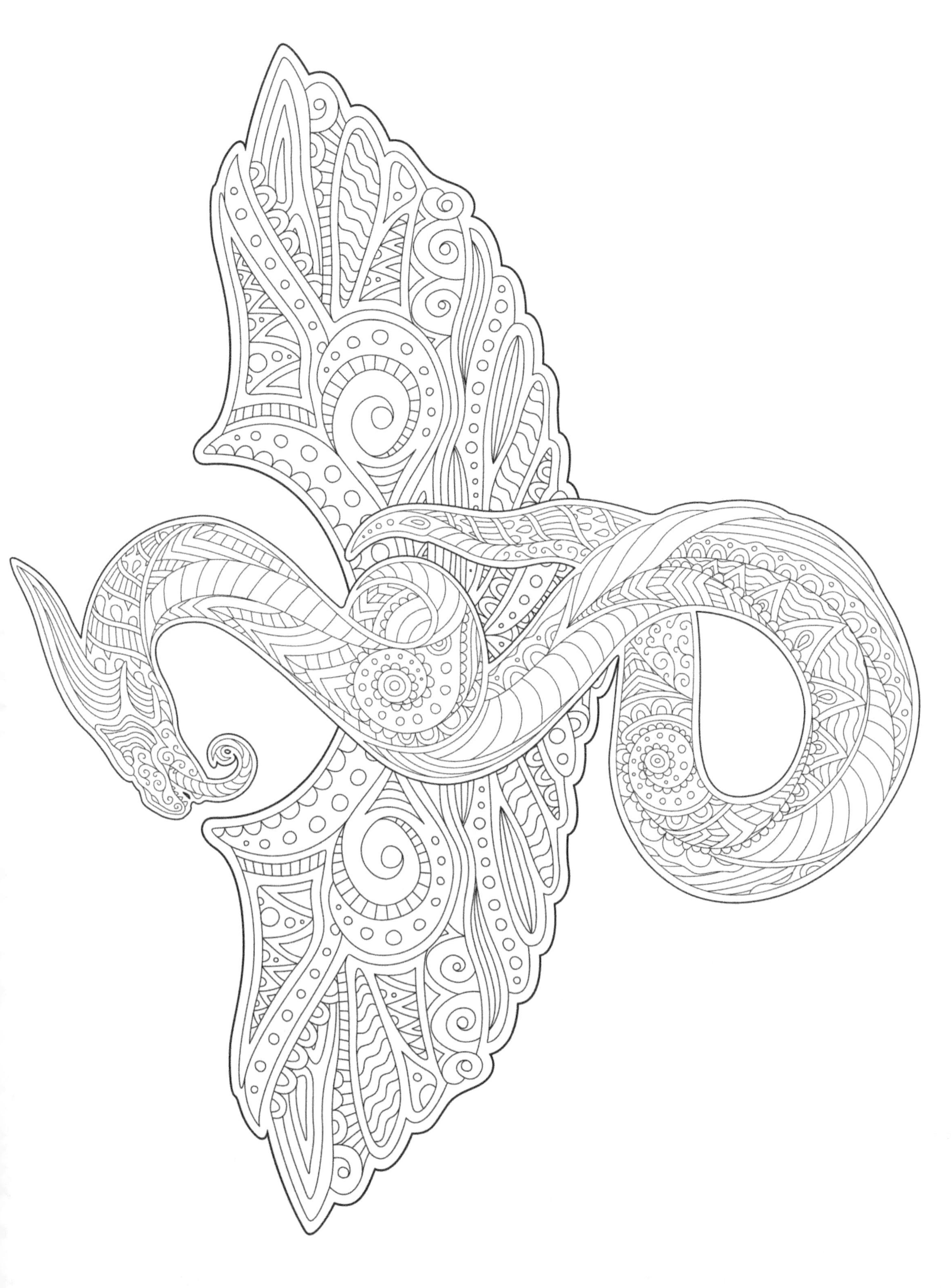

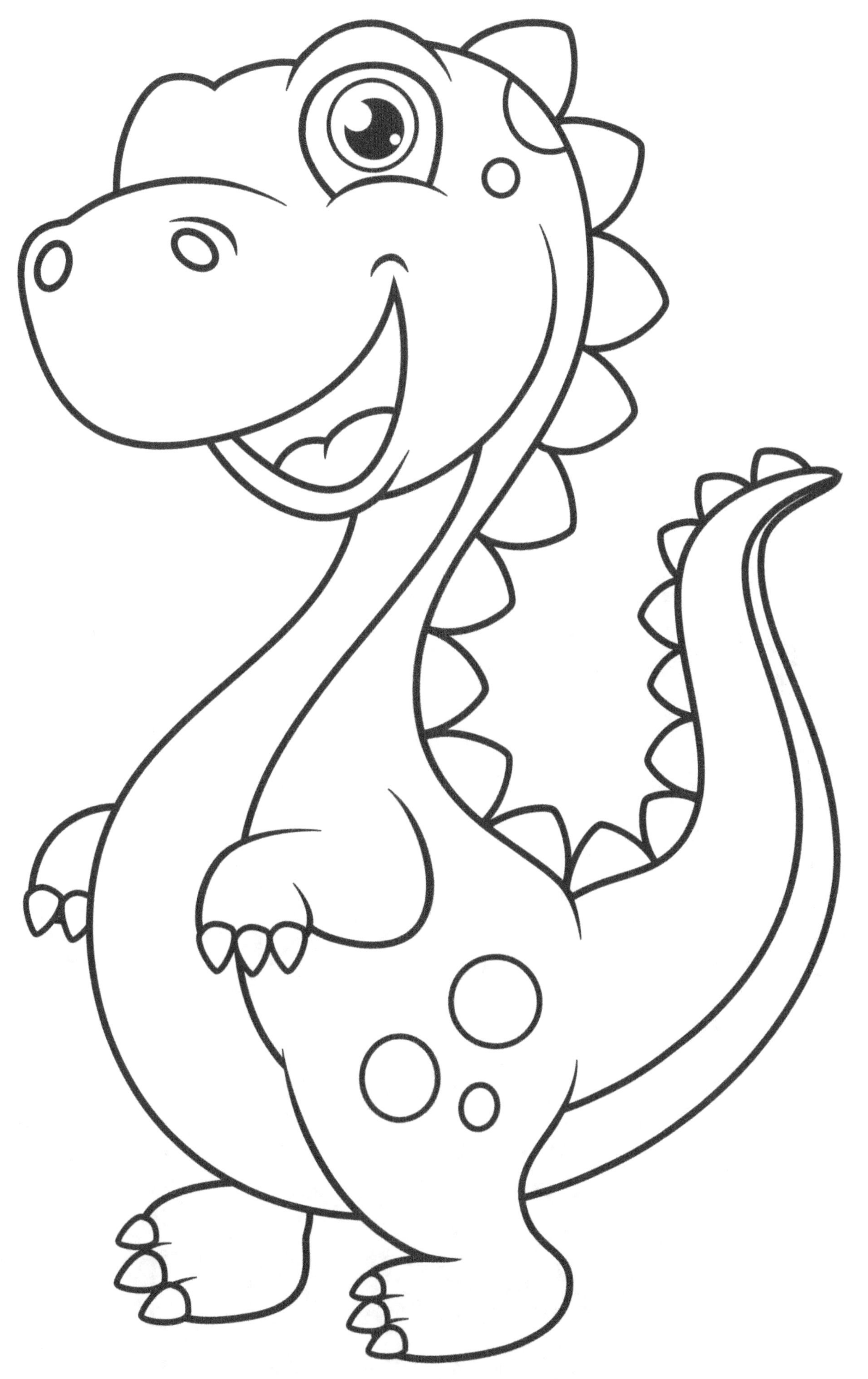

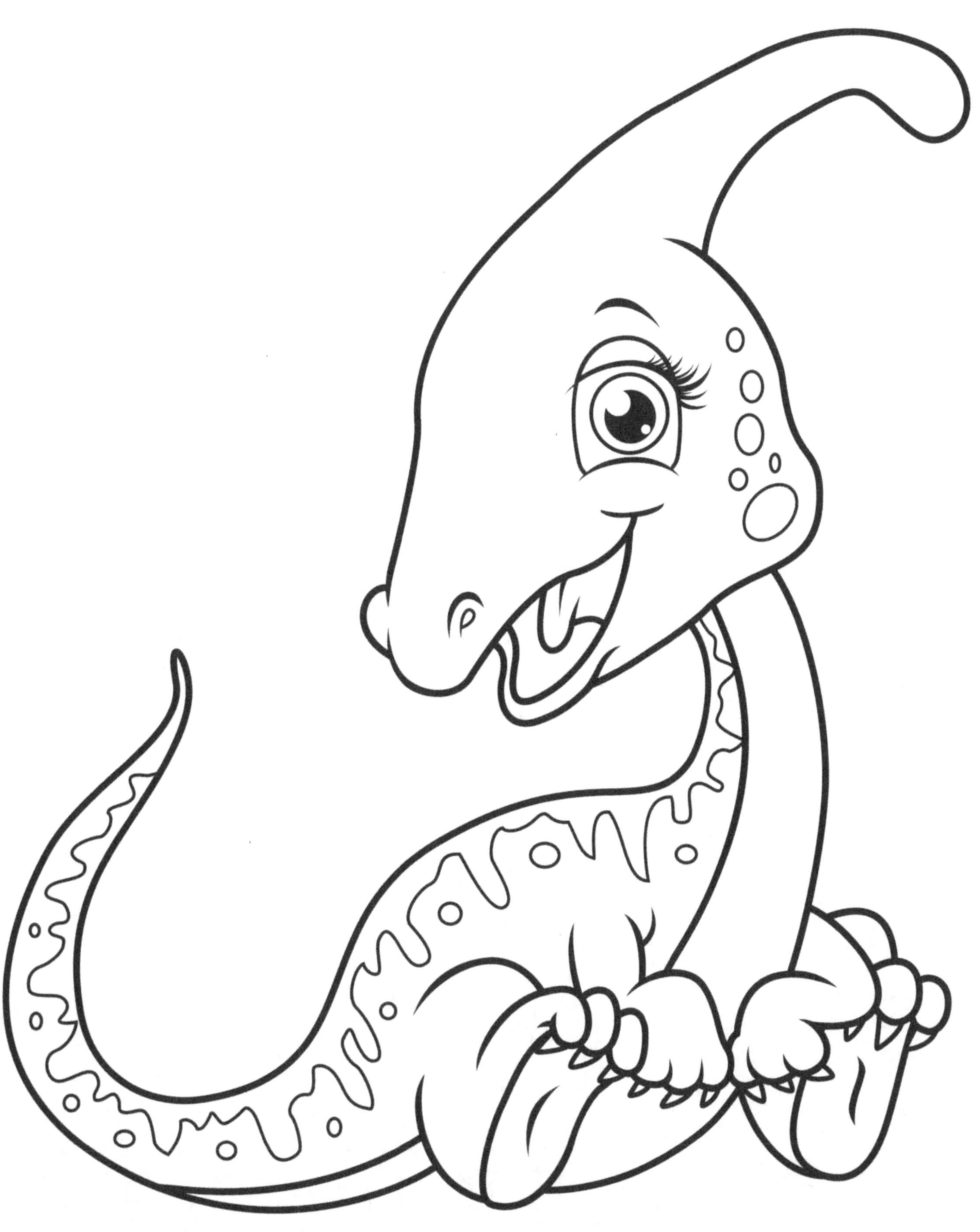

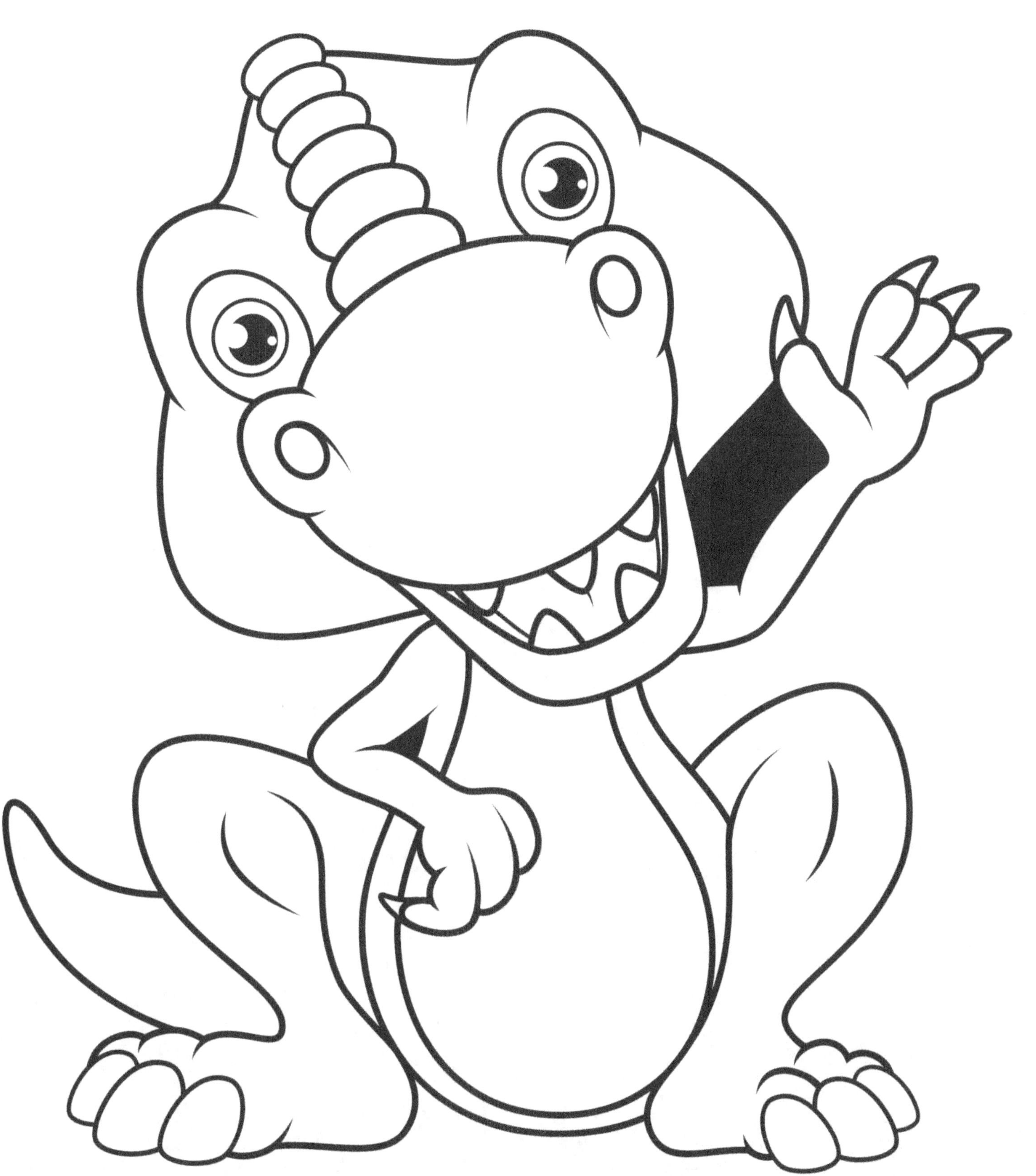